For all princesses, big and small, whose imagination and
creativity transform the world into a magical kingdom. May every stroke of color and every brushstroke be an invitation to explore enchanted tales and create new stories full of sparkle and fantasy. May this book be the portal to a universe where dreams come true and where each page is a kingdom to be discovered. May the magic of art color our days and always remind us of the power that resides within each of us. May princesses at heart be eternal and may the joy of coloring accompany us forever.

With love,
Lara

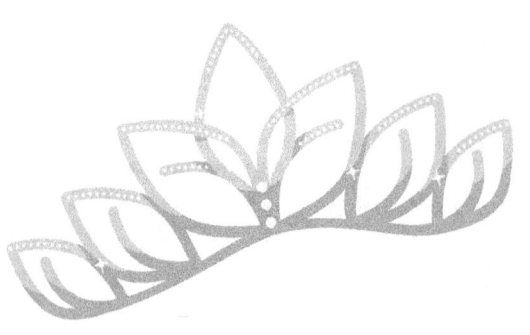

THIS BOOK BELONGS TO:

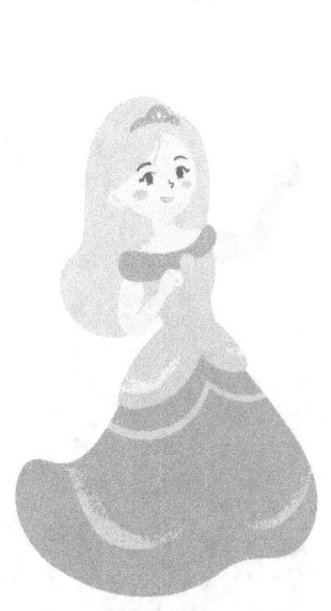
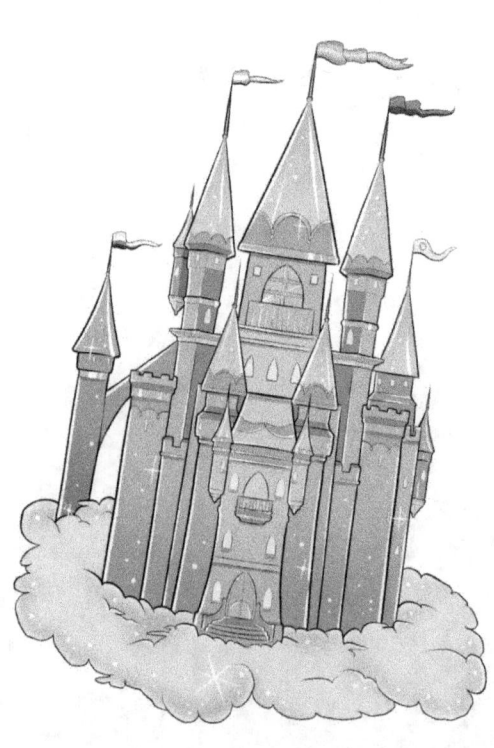

ALL RIGHTS RESERVED ©
2024

No part of this publication may be reproduced, distributed, or transmitted in any form or by any means, including photocopying, recording, or other electronic or mechanical methods, without the prior written permission of the publisher, except for brief quotations incorporated in critical reviews and other specific noncommercial uses. Any unauthorized replica of this work is prohibited.

L.P.T ©
Lara Perguer Tramontin

Test color page

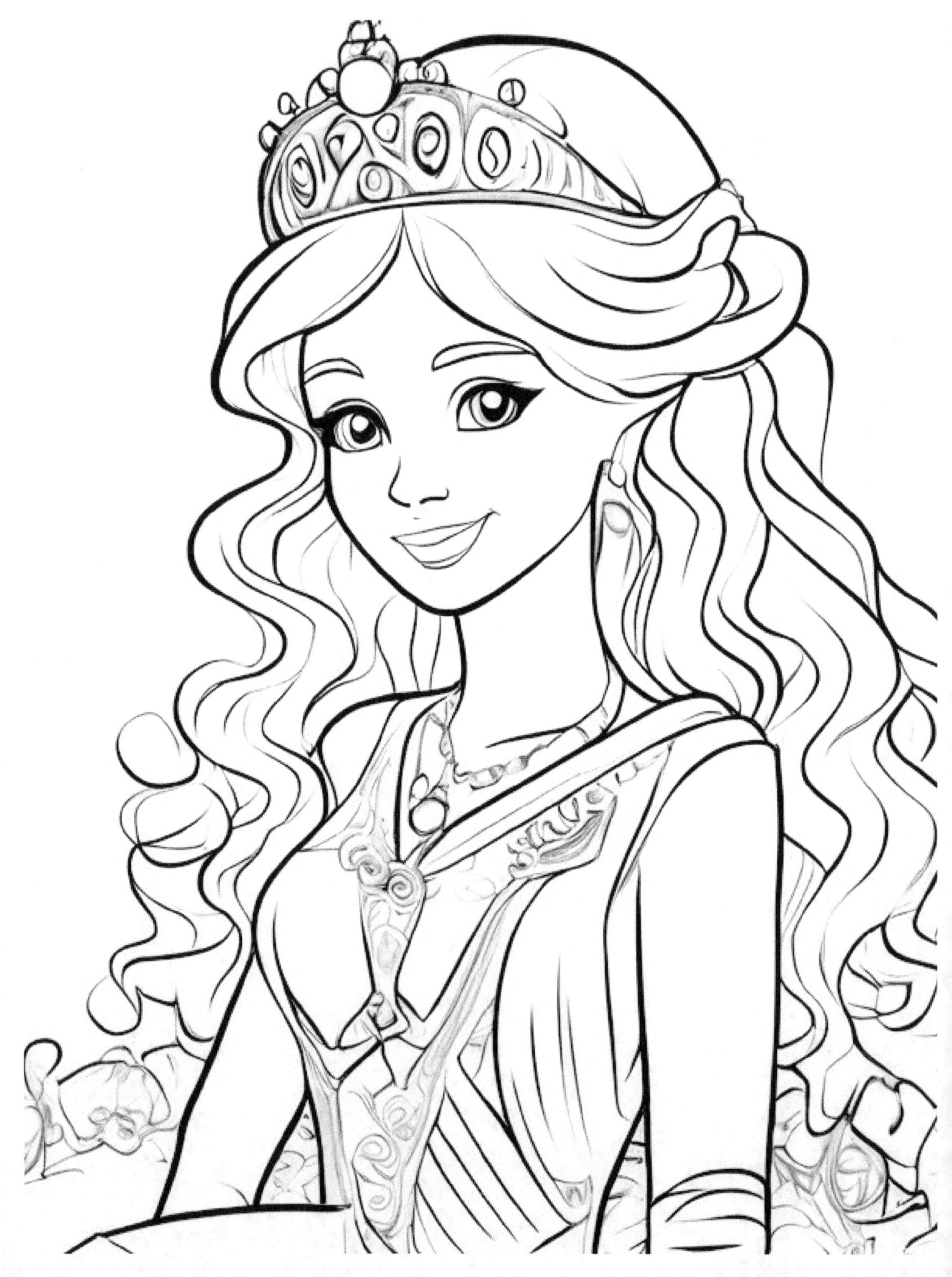

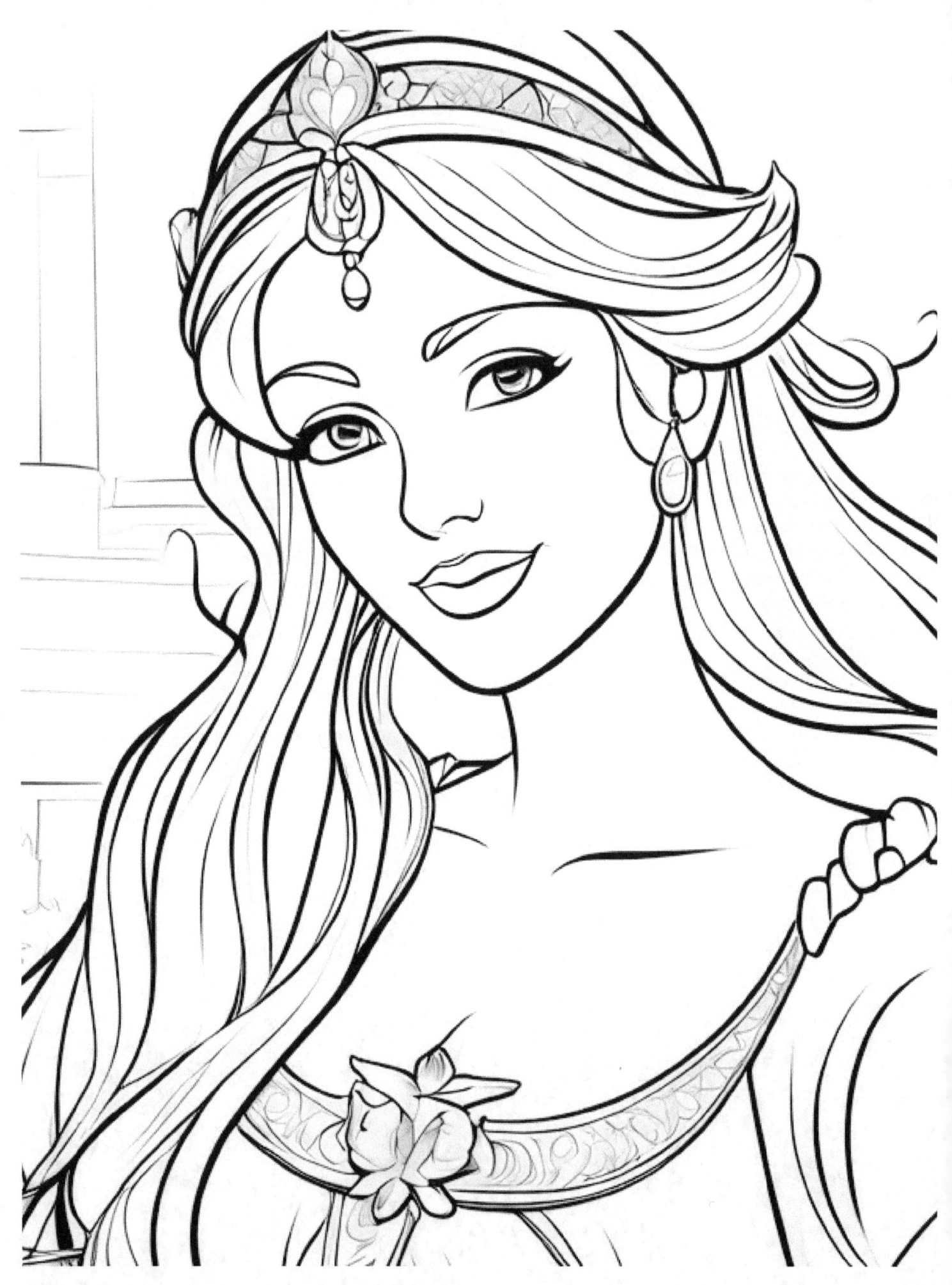

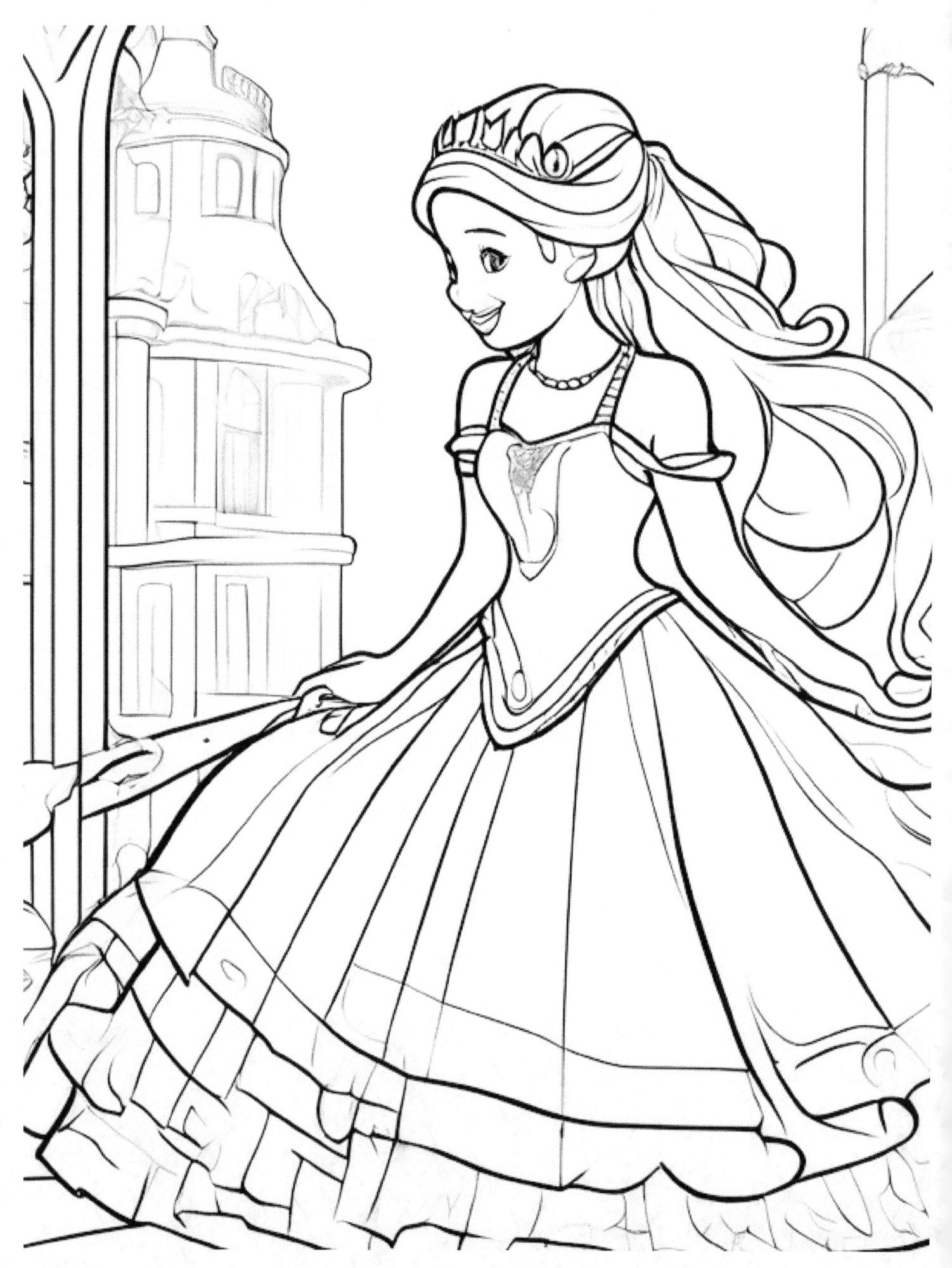

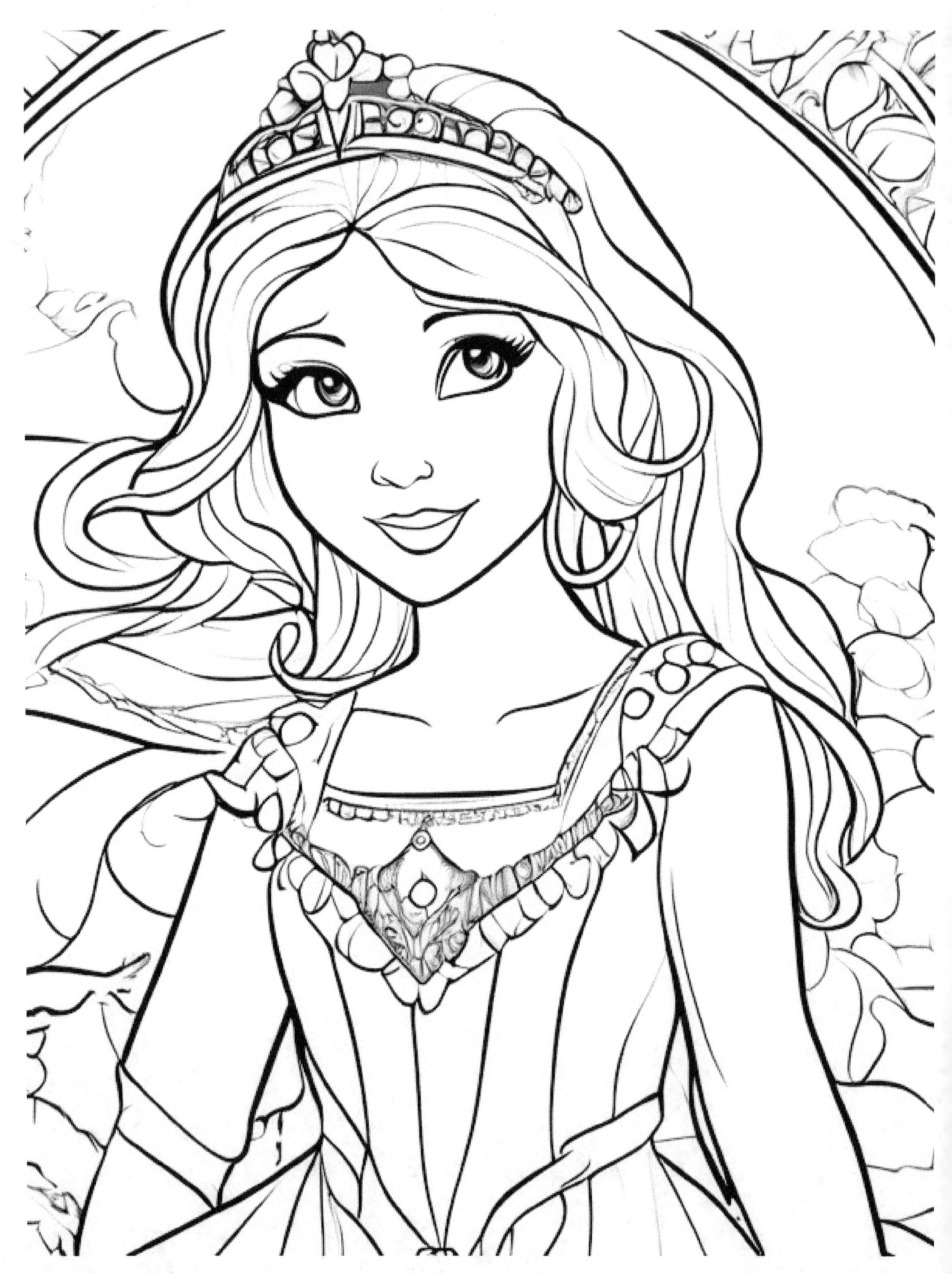

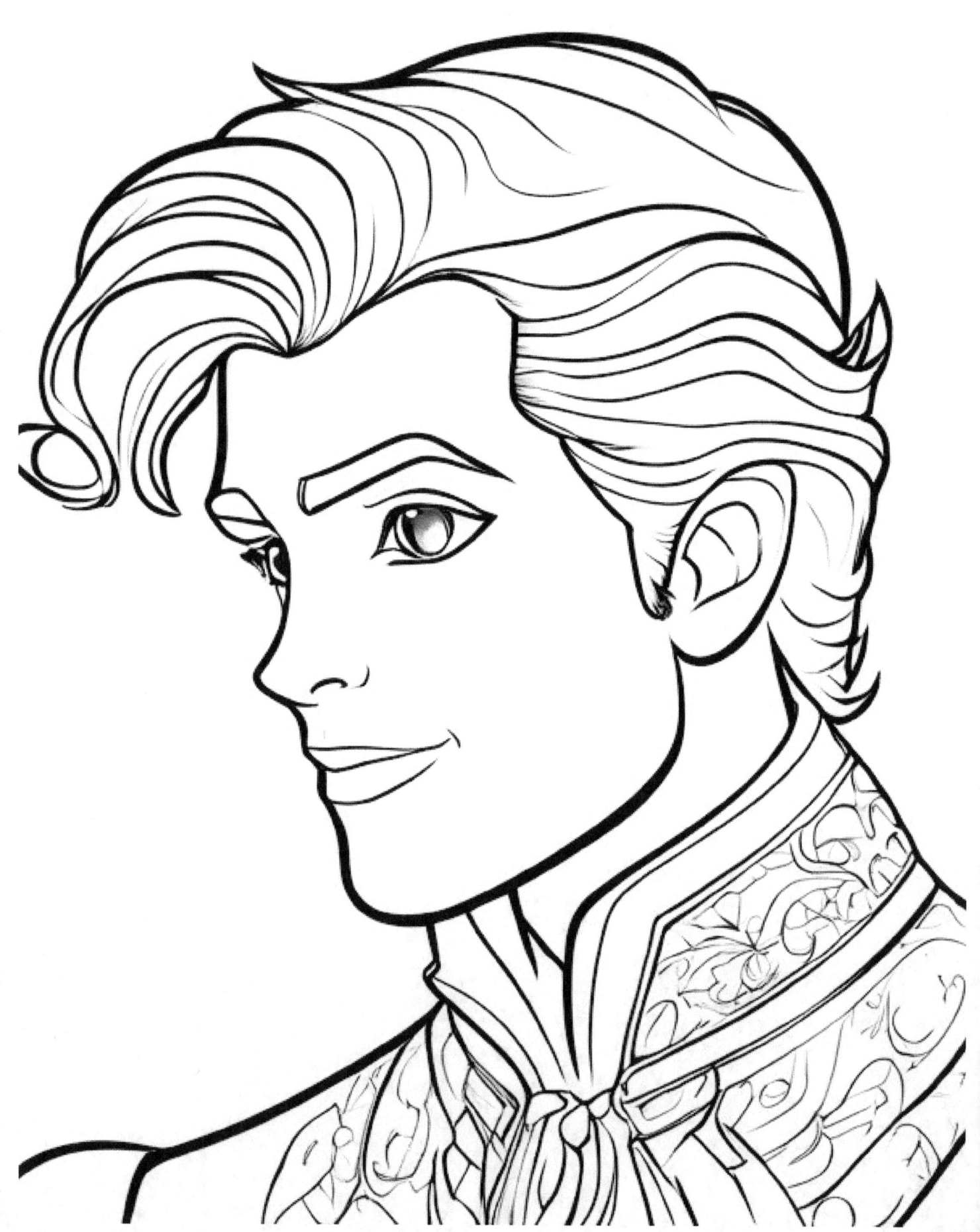

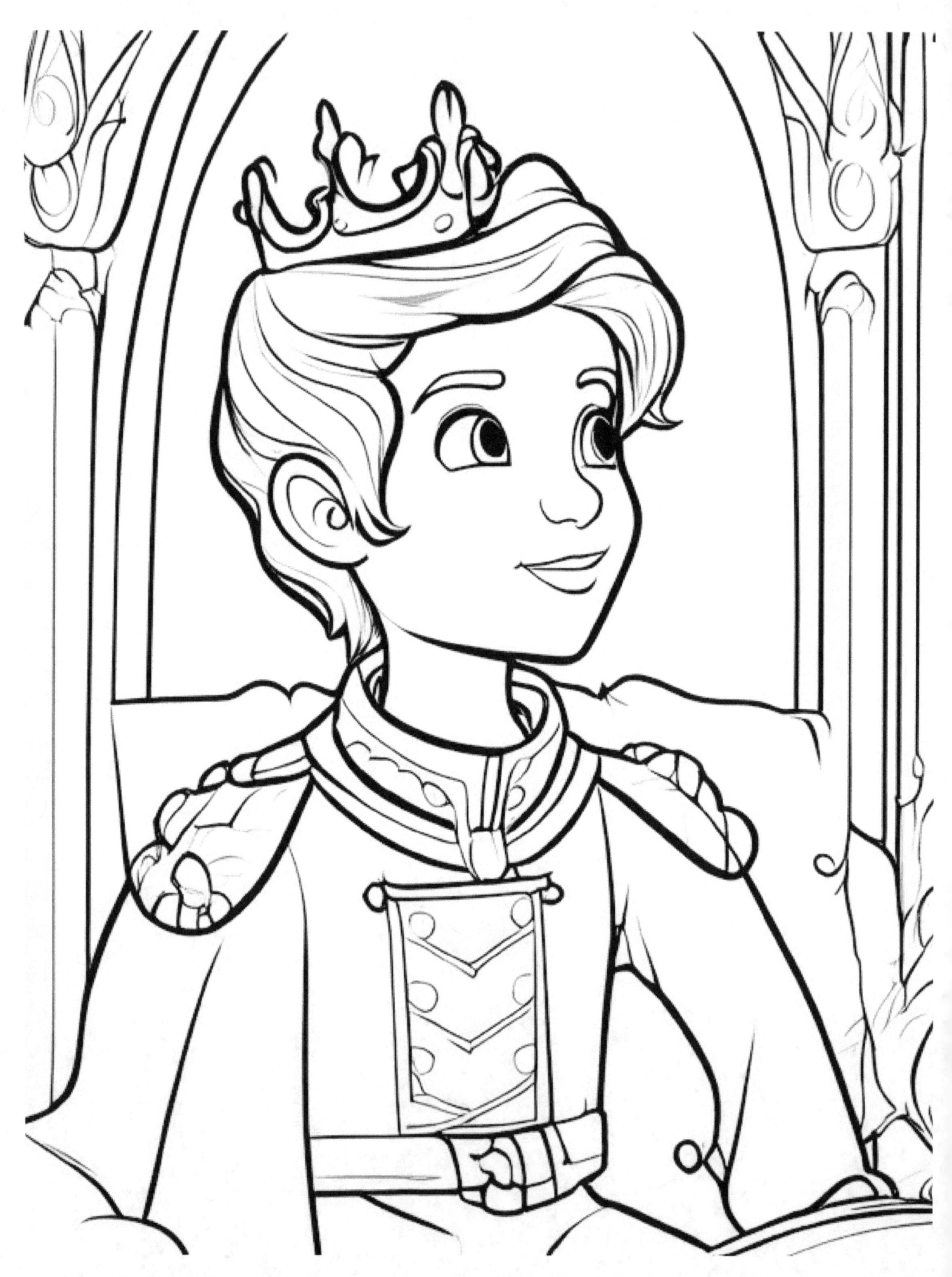

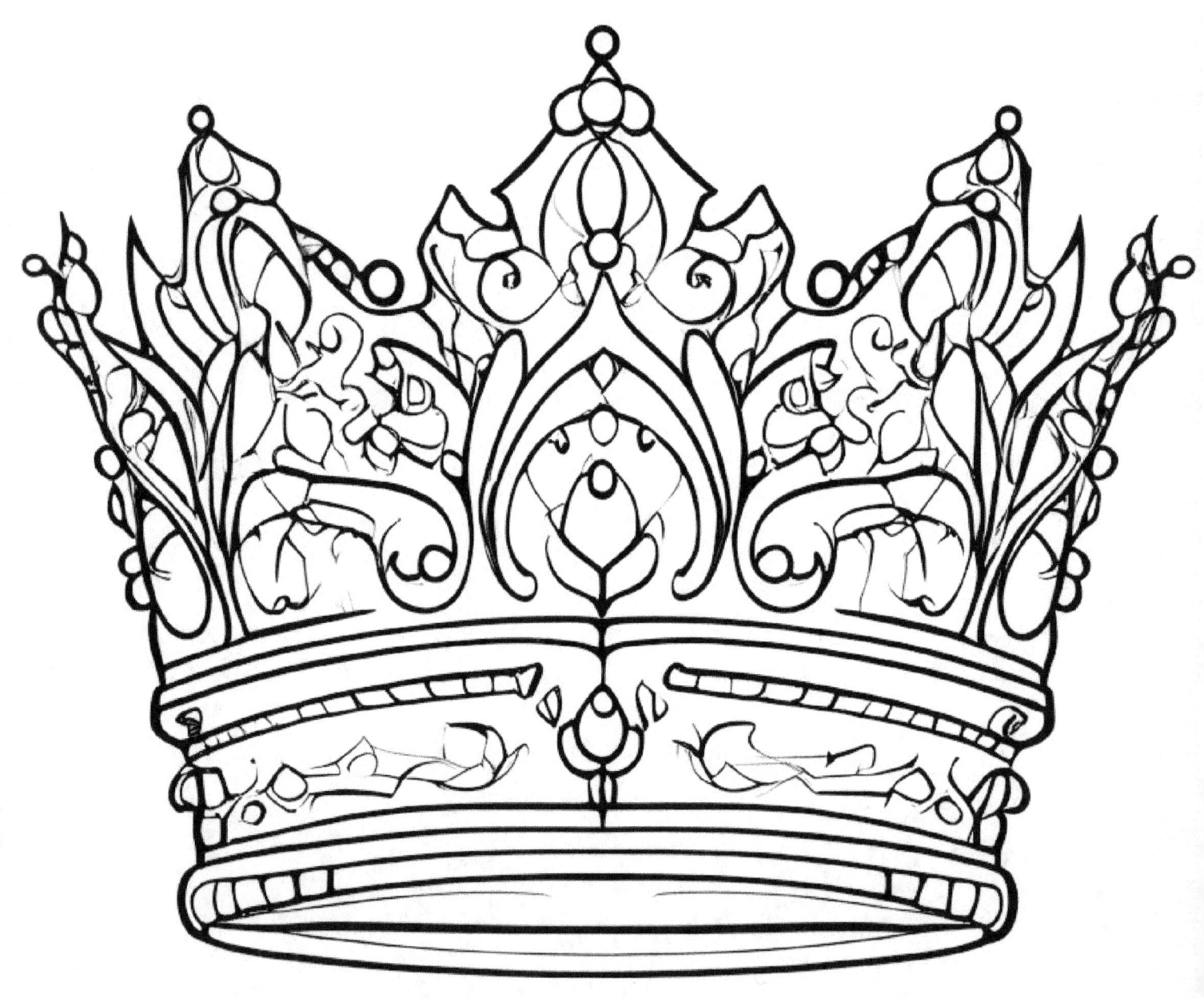

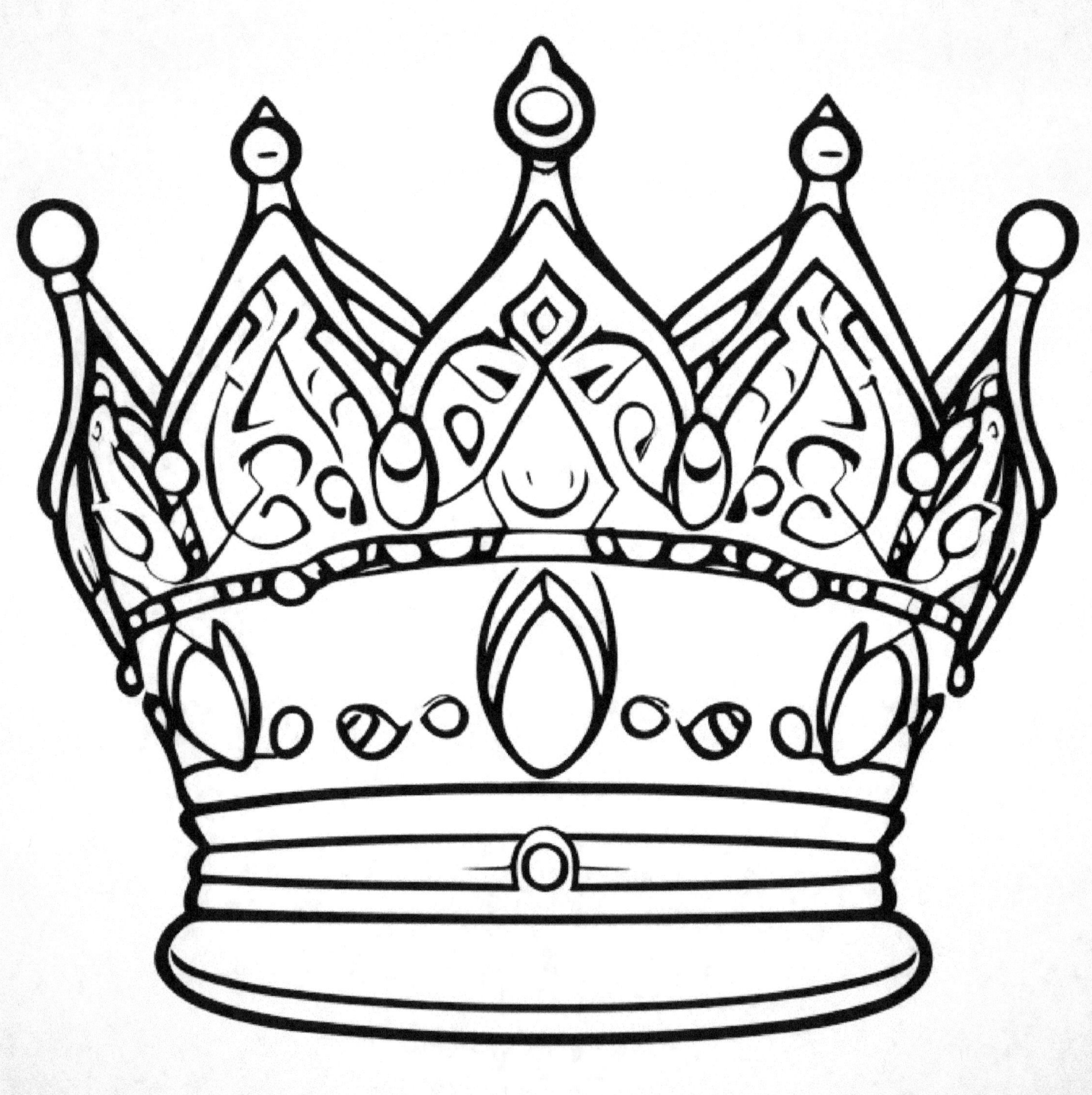

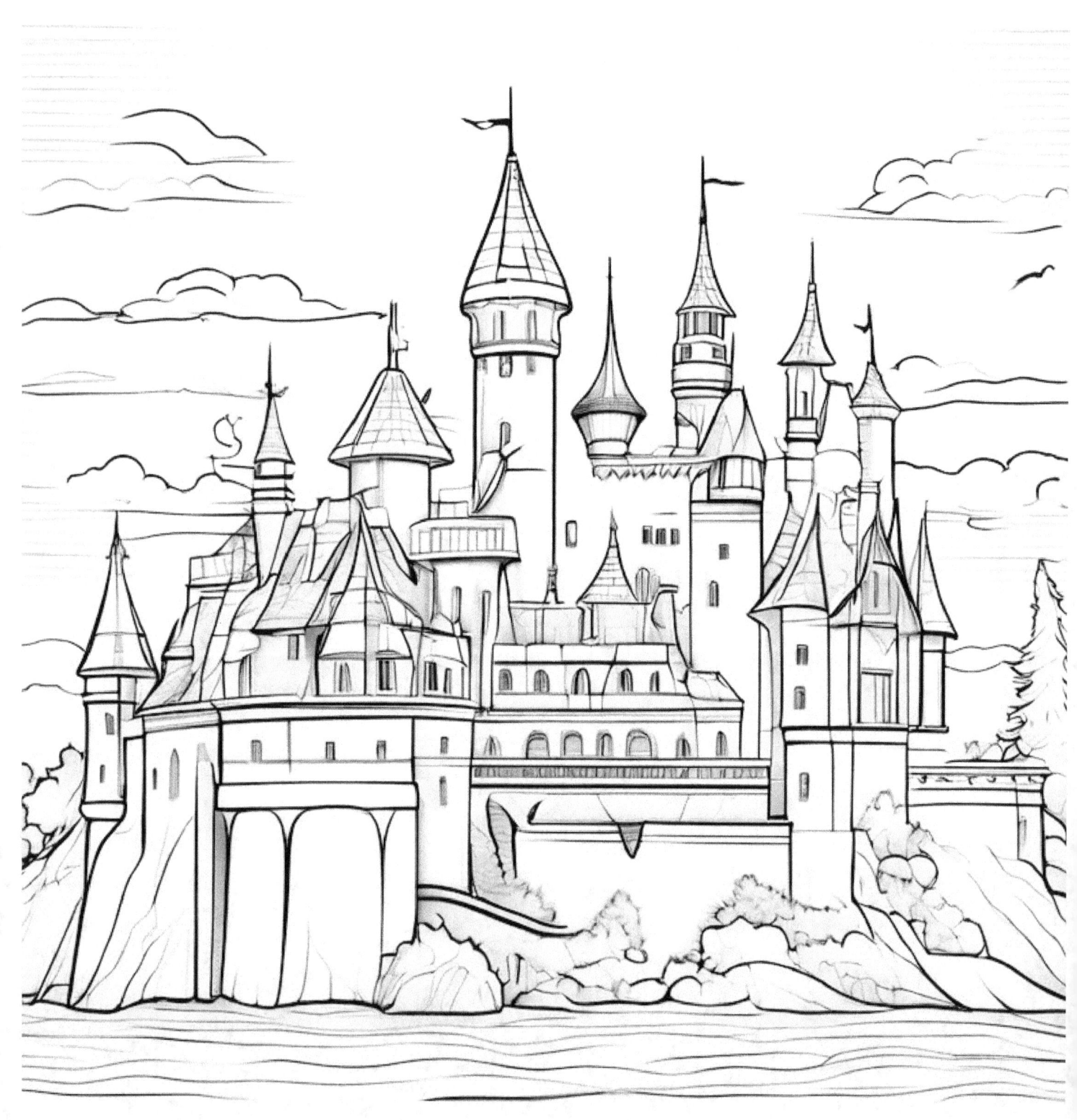

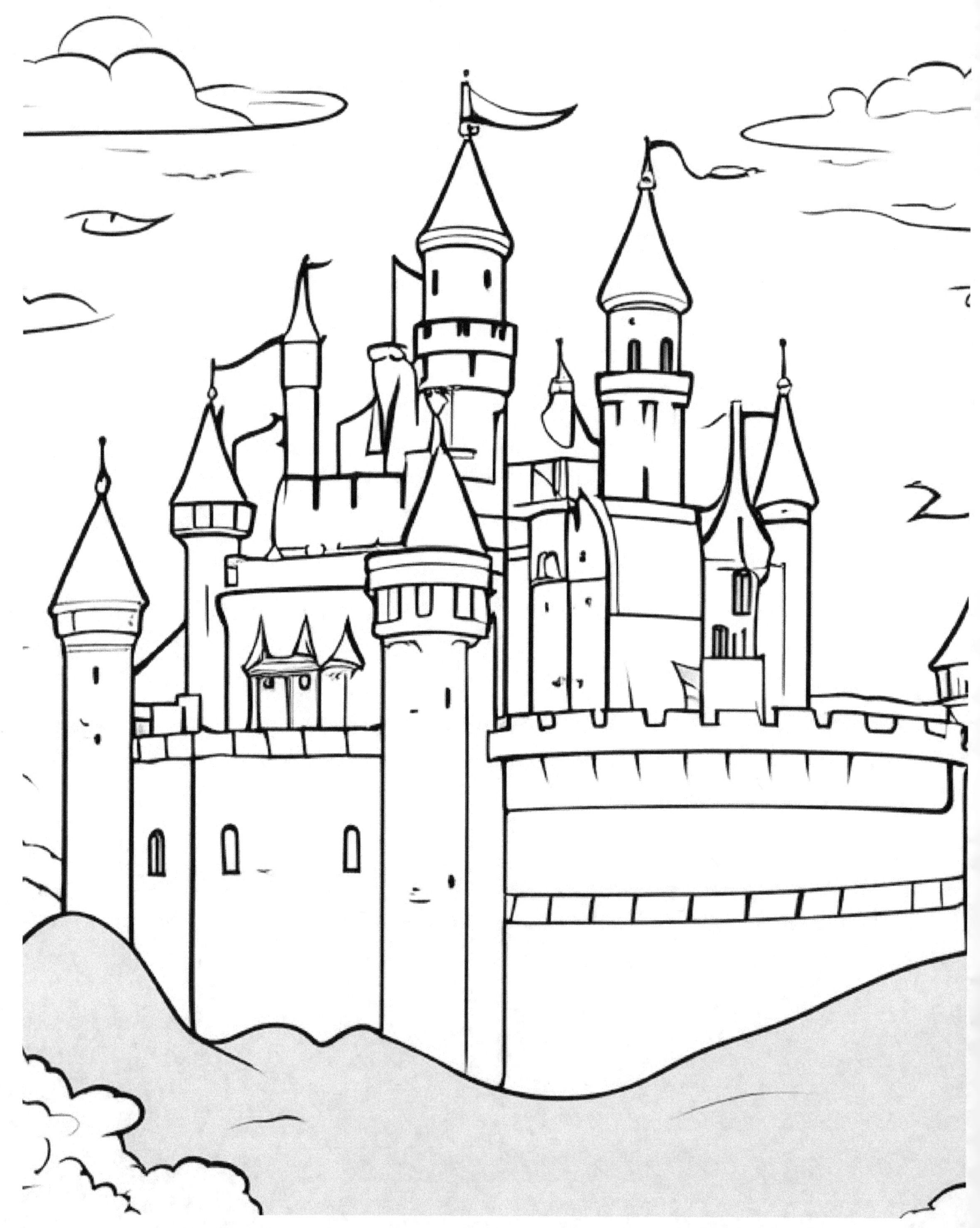

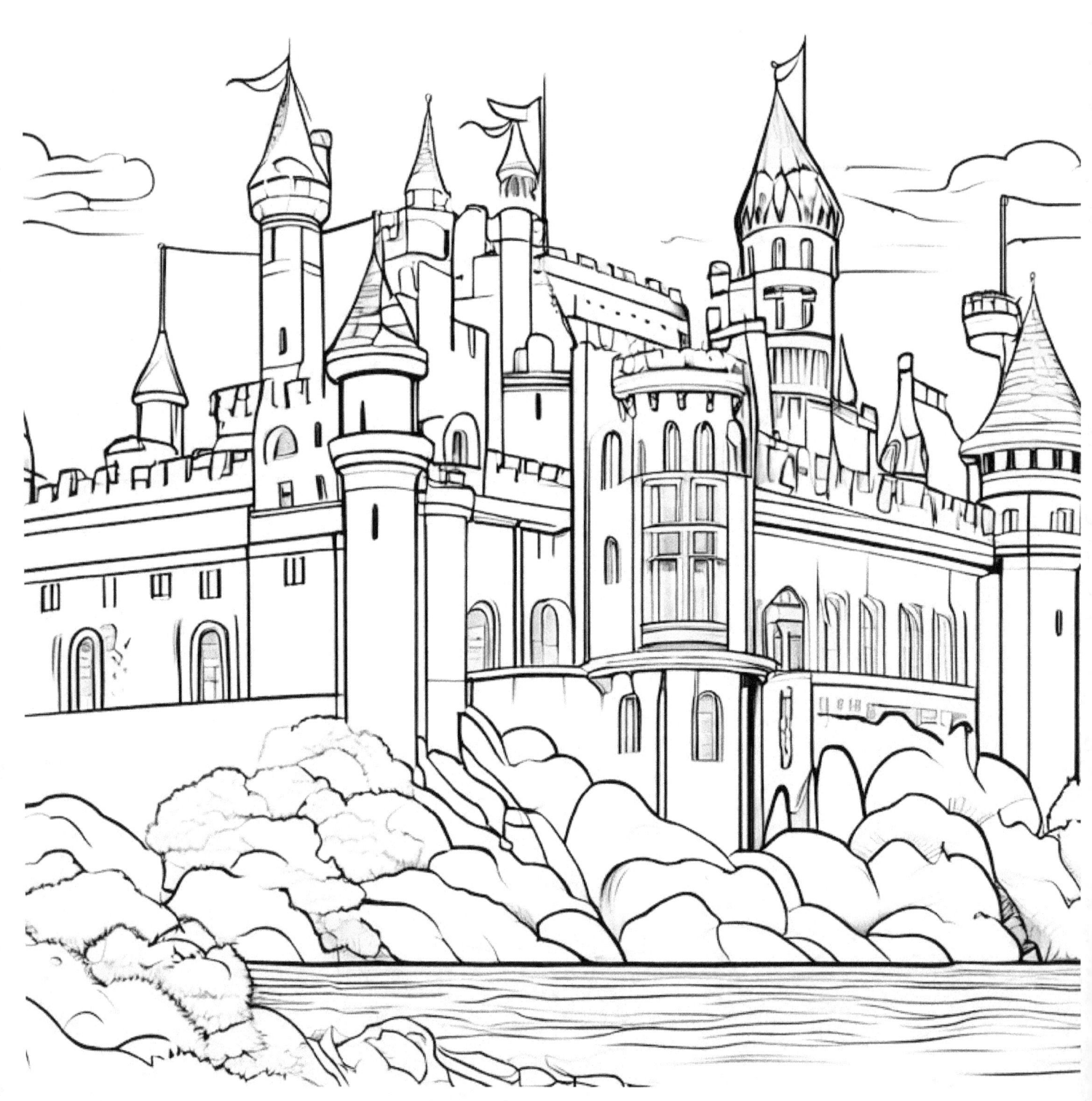

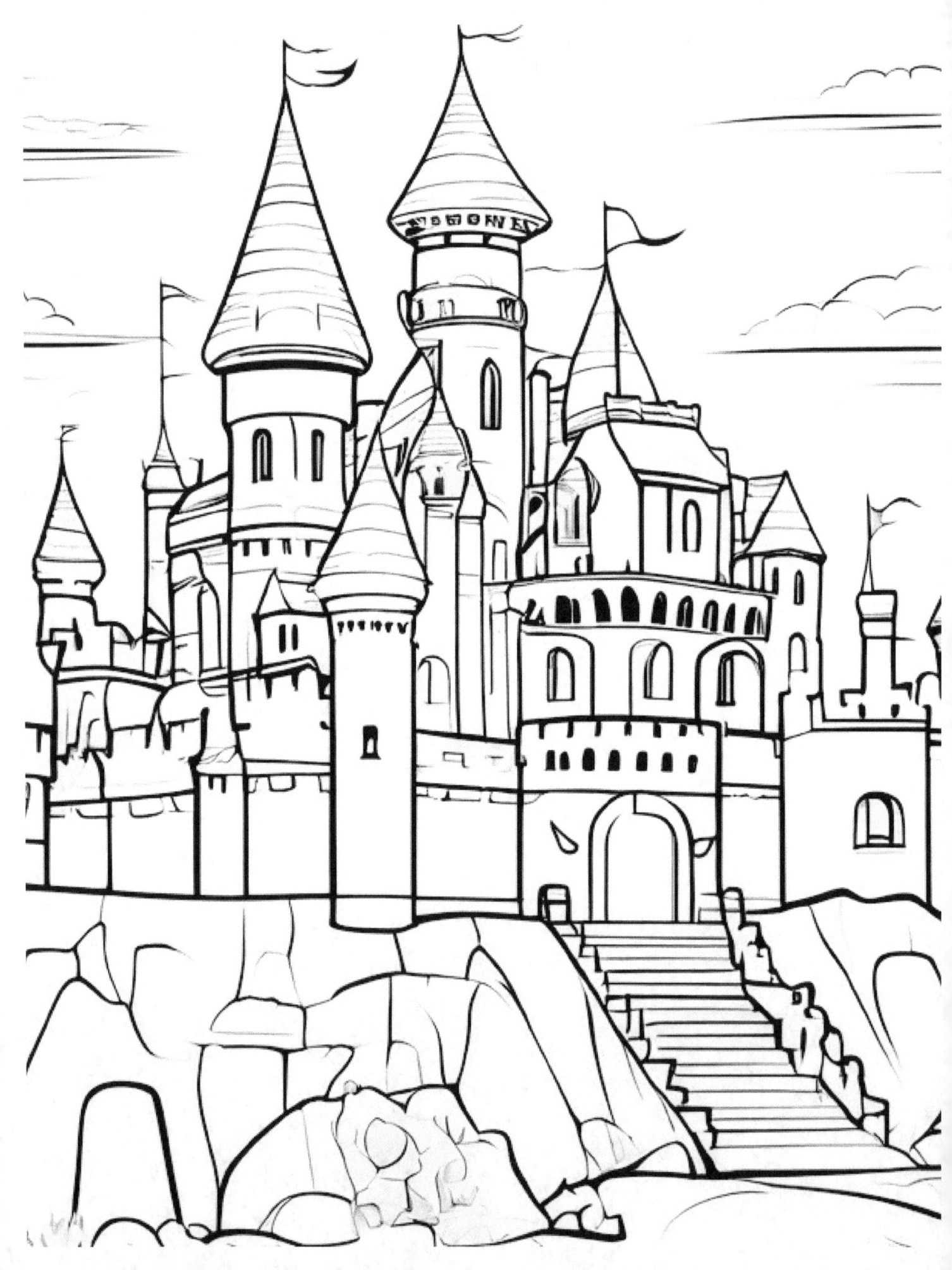

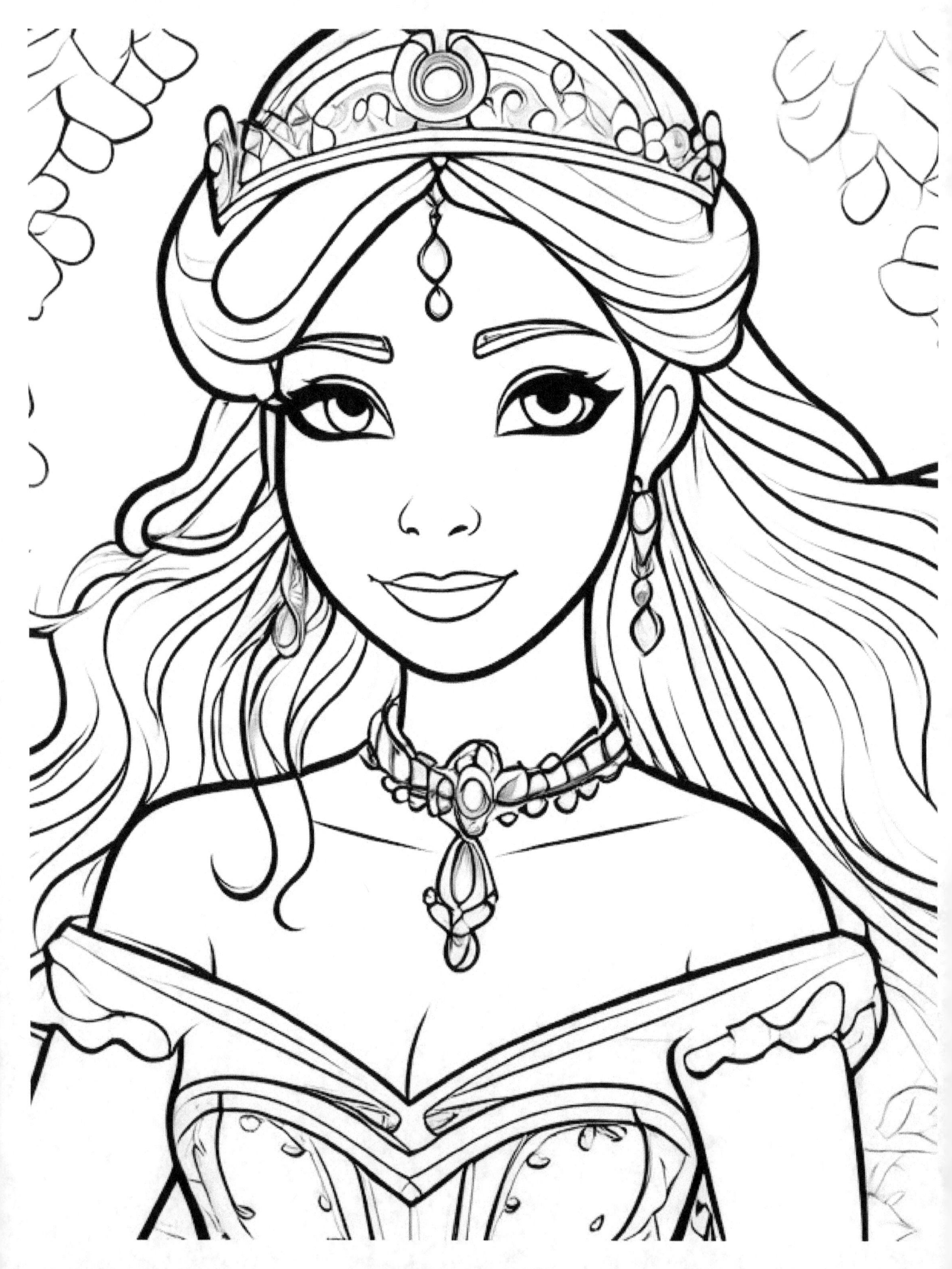

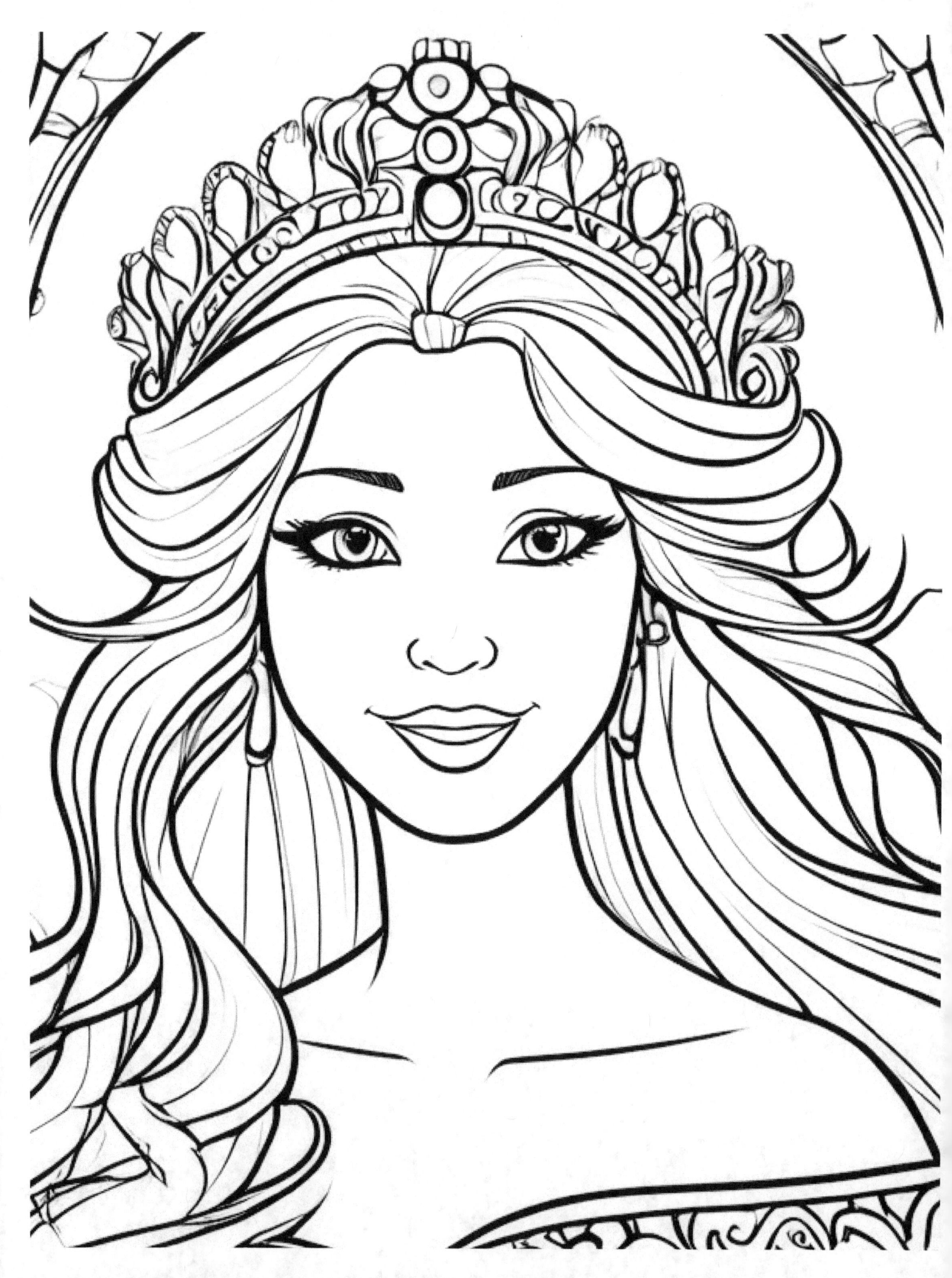

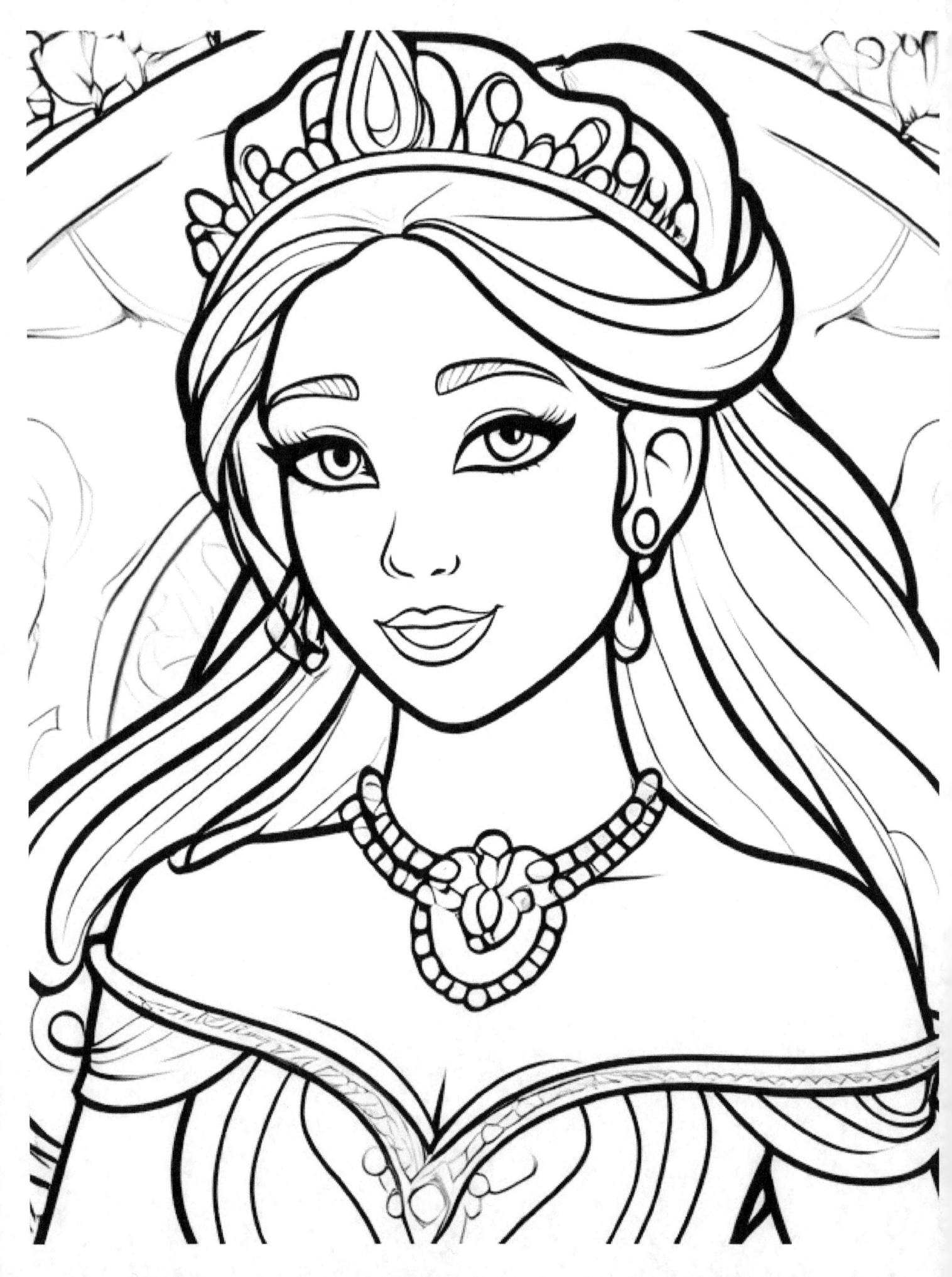

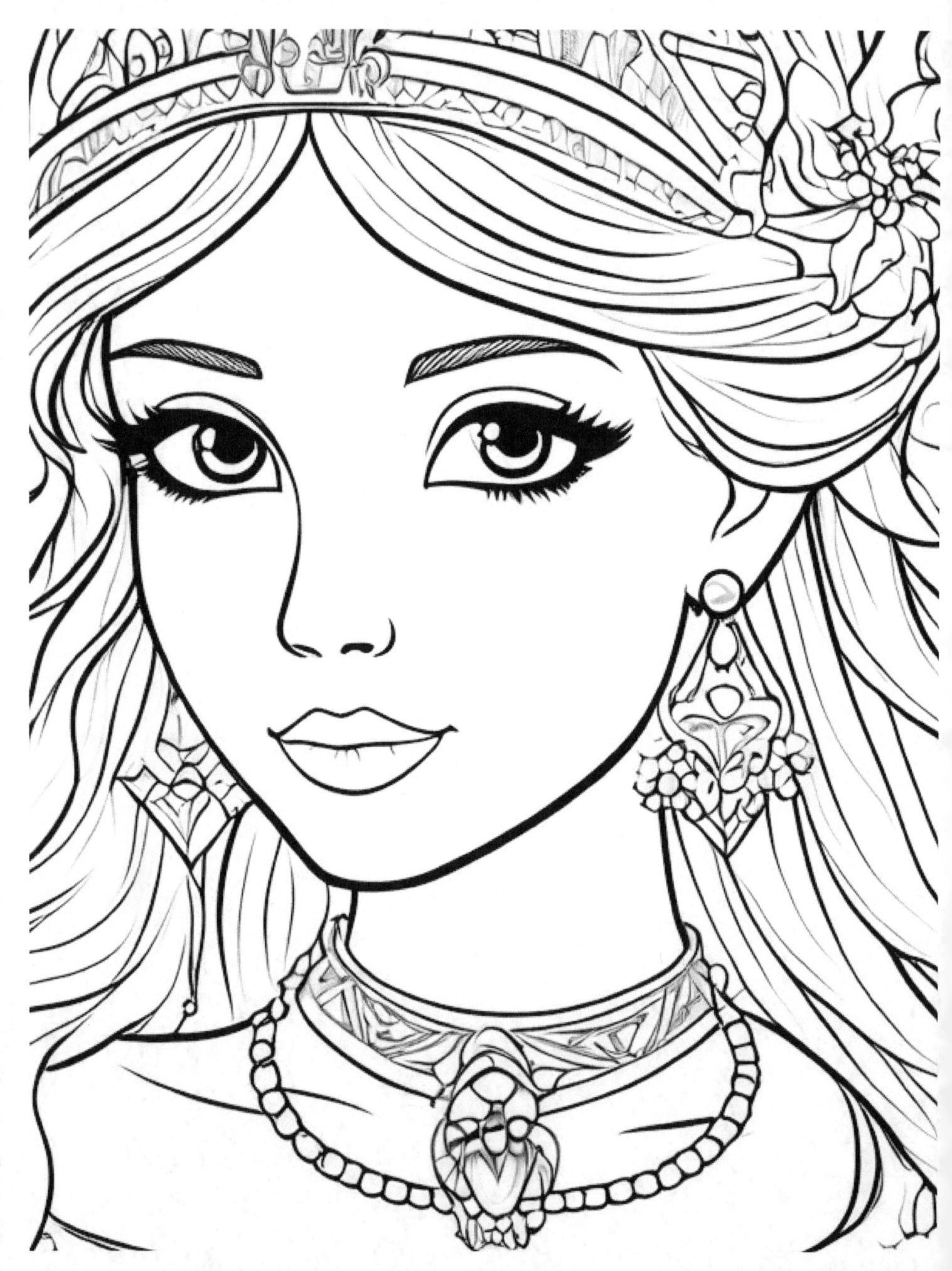

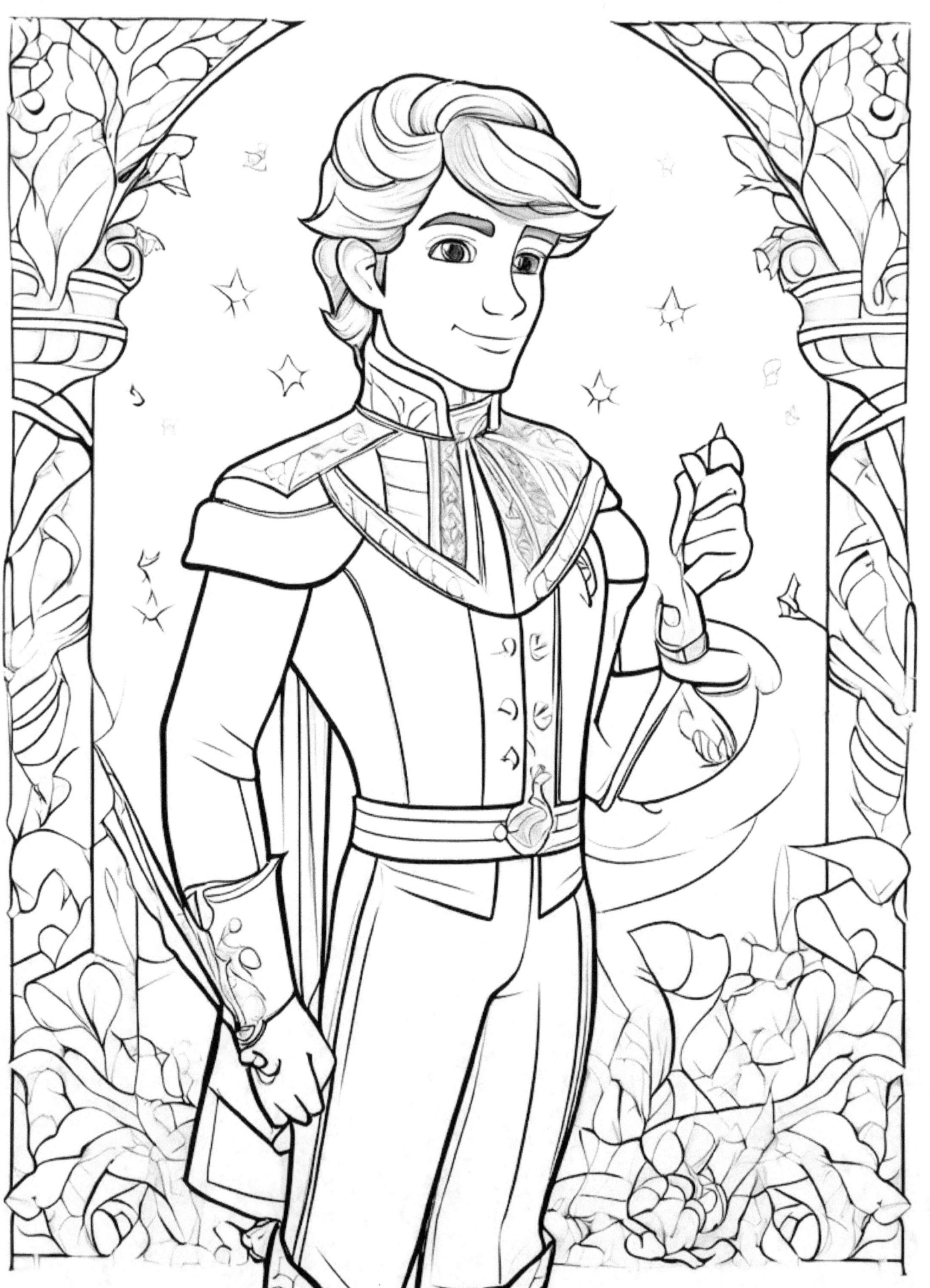

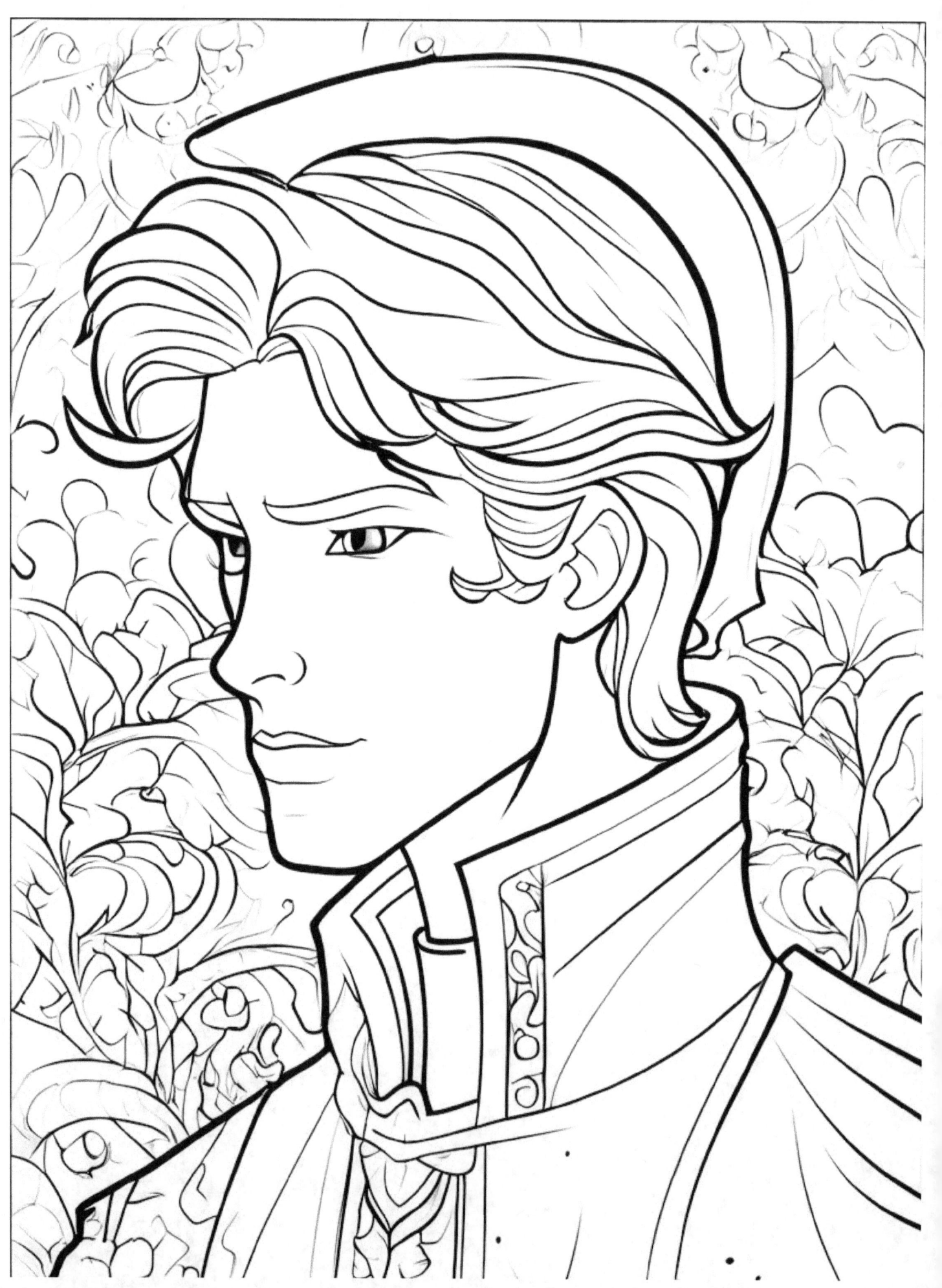

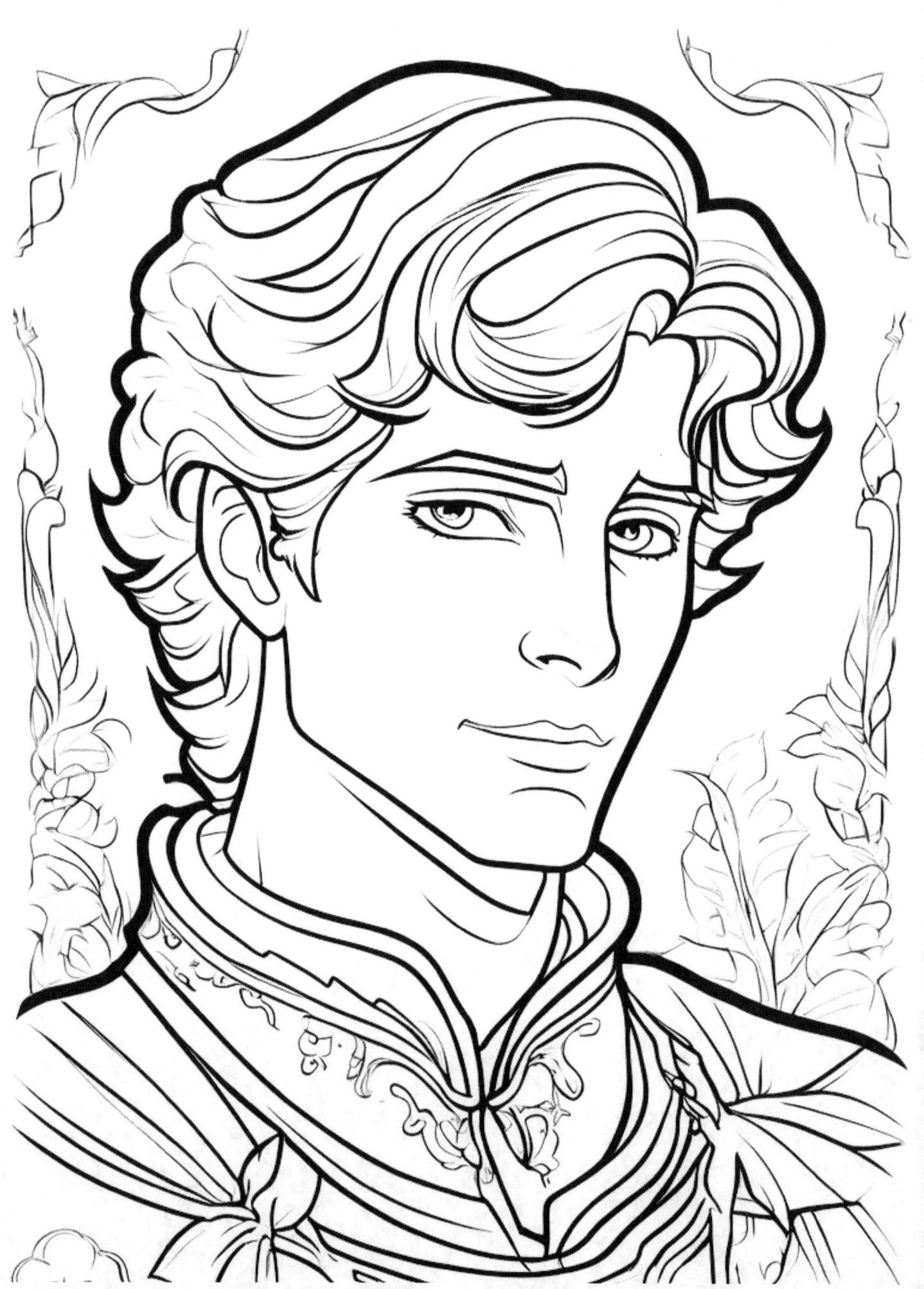

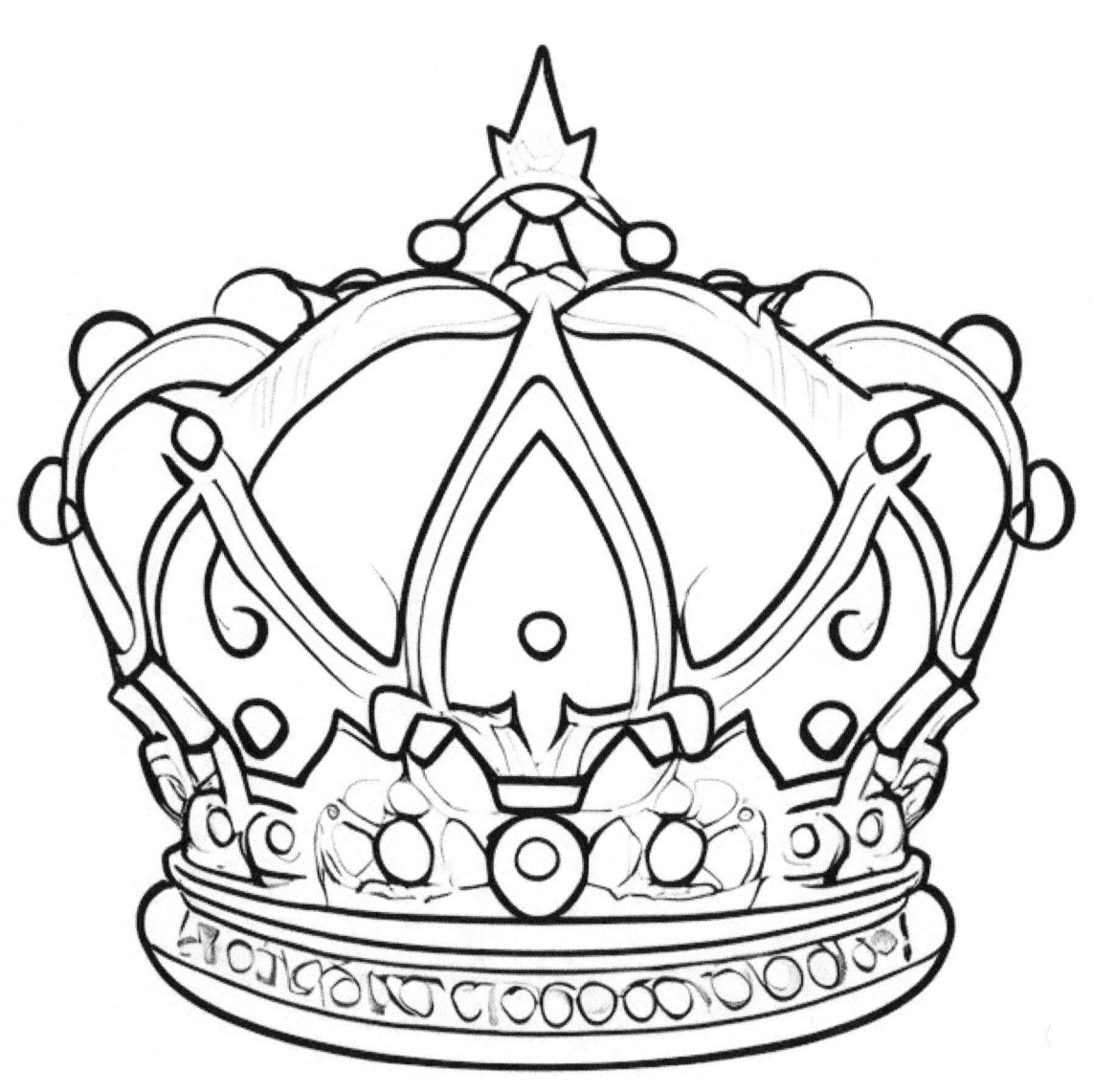

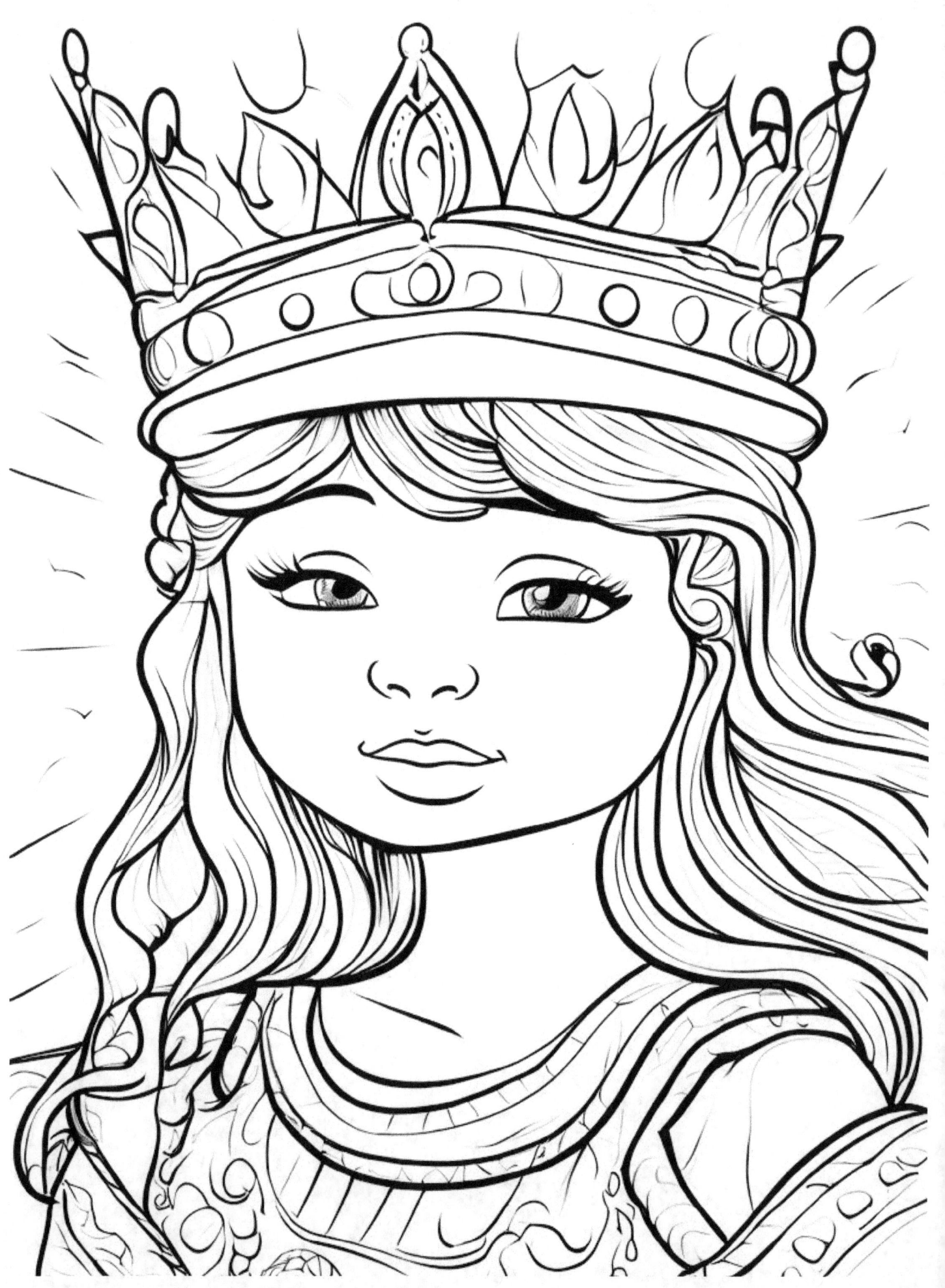

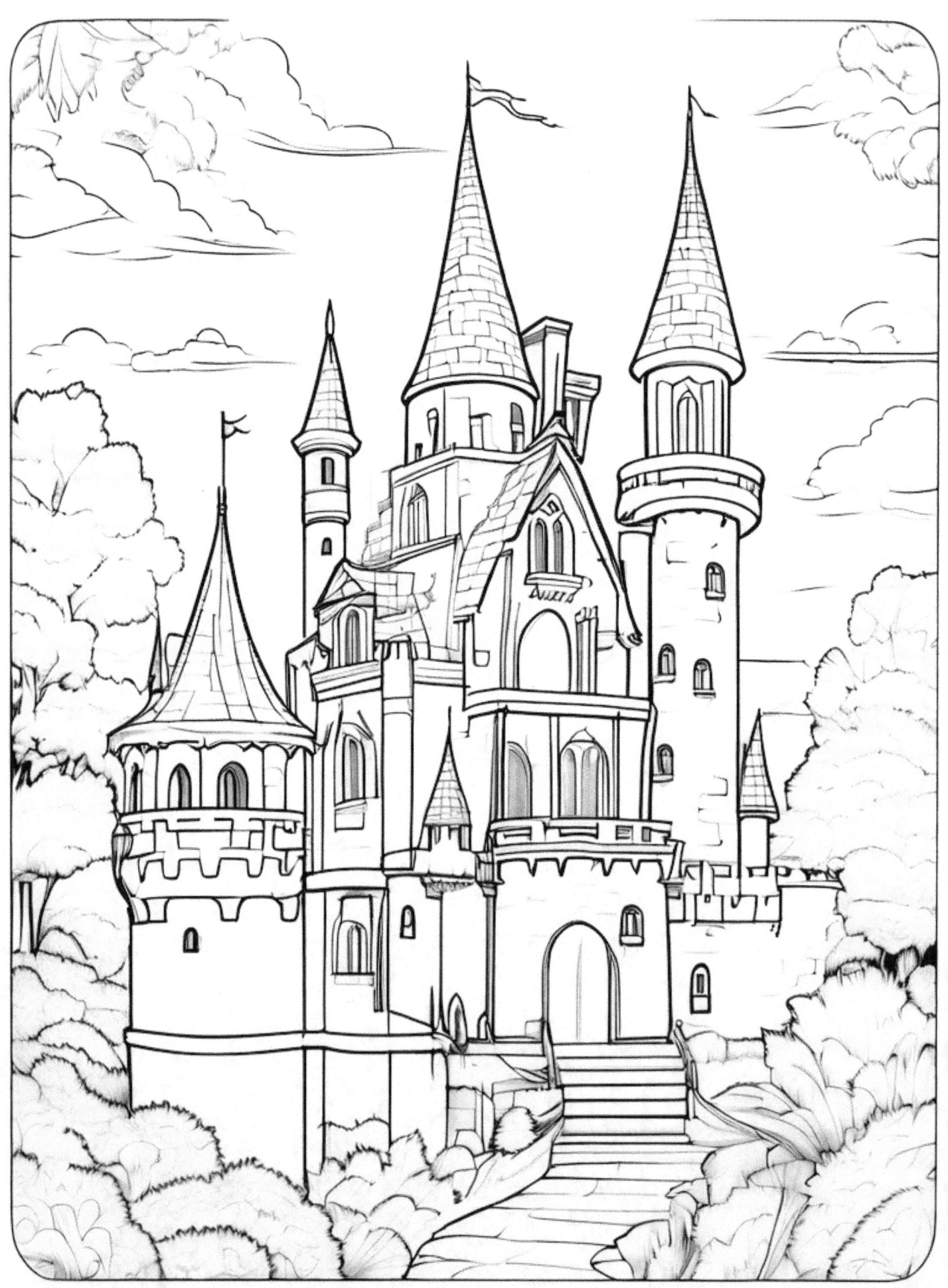

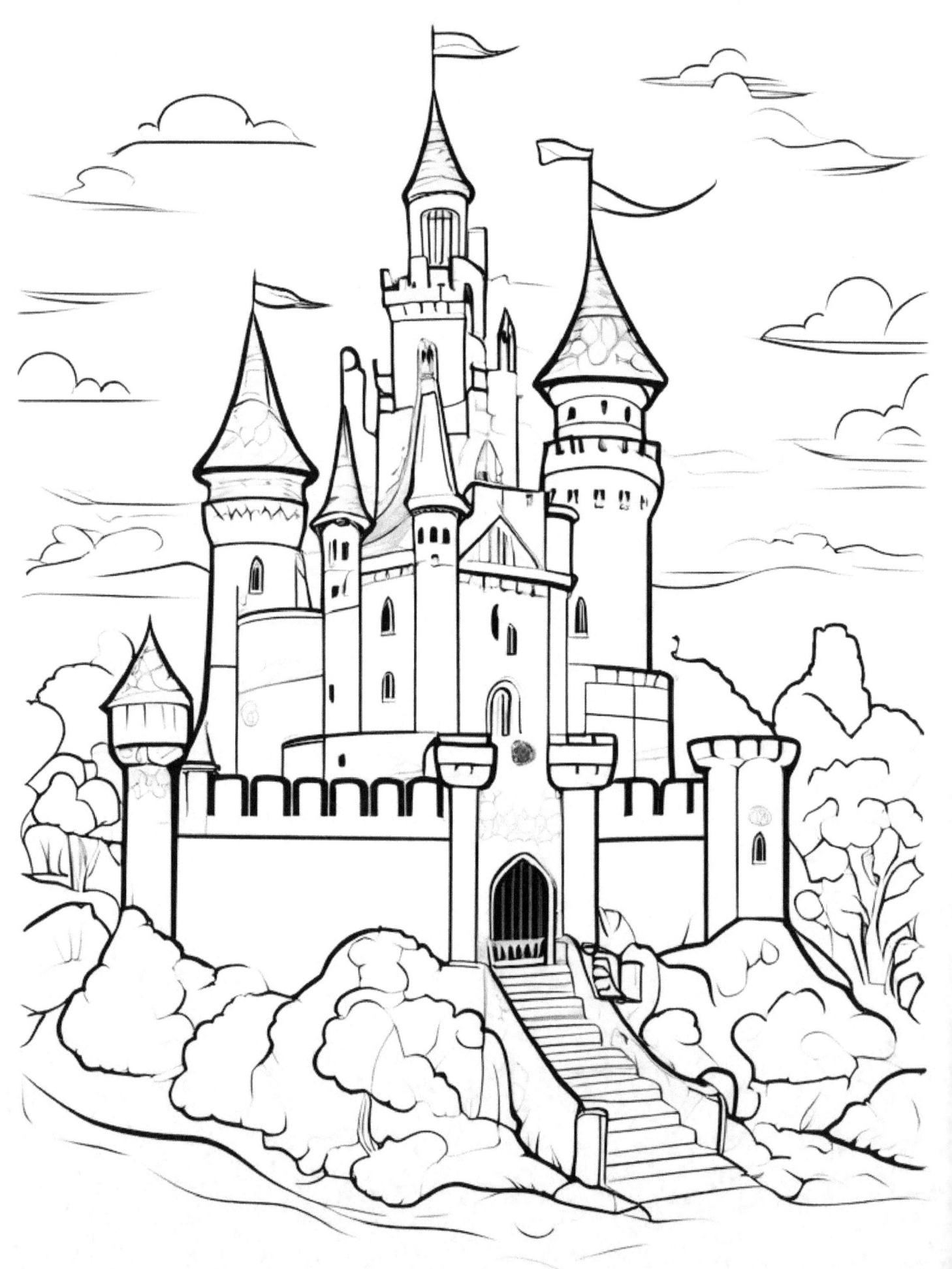

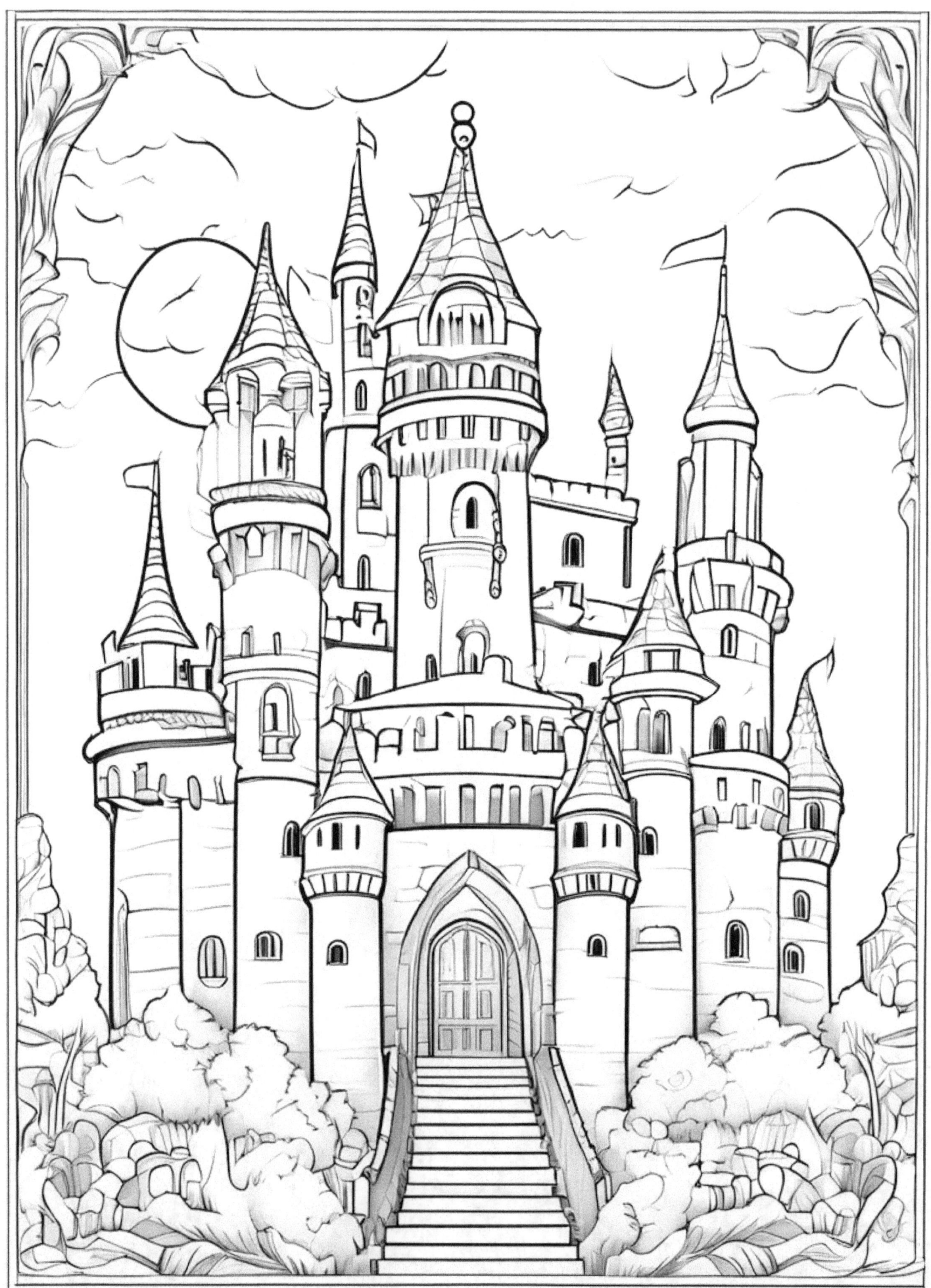